Sweet Dreams and Time for Bed

by **Tish Rabe**

illustrated by **Gill Guile**

To Solfen + Caulder,
Have fun reading,
best wishes,
Tish Rabe

© 2021 Tish Rabe Books, LLC. ALL RIGHTS RESERVED.

It's time for us
to end our day

Time to tuck the day away

Now the sun is going to sleep

Splish! Splash! Soapy hands and feet

Show me how
you brush your teeth

Cozy pajamas
soft and snug

Special friend to give a hug

Storybooks you like the best

Time for you to get some rest

Snuggle down
   inside your bed

       Gentle kisses
          on your head

              Dream sweet dreams
                 and when you do

Know now and always...

I **love** you

**As the day ends,
there are things you can do
to make sleep better
for your children and for you.**

- ♥ Thirty to sixty minutes before you tuck them in
  is a good time for their bedtime routine to begin

- ♥ You can show them how to put away
  some of the things that filled their day

- ♥ To help them shift from day to night,
  turn off screens with noise and light

- ♥ Slow things down and you will find
  they'll start to relax, calm down, unwind

- ♥ Read books your children love most of all,
  or tell them stories about you when you were small

"When I was a little turtle, I lived on an island far, far away."

**It's fun to ask questions
as you read along
because any answers are right
and no answers are wrong.**

- ♥ What was your favorite part of today?

- ♥ If you could be any animal in this bedtime story, who would you be? Why?

- ♥ What do you put away before you go to bed?

- ♥ Which storybooks do you like to read the most?

- ♥ I wonder what we will do tomorrow. What do you think?

"Once upon a time, there was a bunny who was very brave — just like you."

The sound of your voice when you read and sing is what your child loves more than anything.

A Sweet Dreams Lullaby

Sing to the tune of "Twinkle, Twinkle Little Star"

Night is here, today is done
It's time to sleep my little one

Now it's time to feel the day
softly, slowly slip away

Tomorrow will be bright and new,
and I will share it all with you

Now the sky's lit by the moon
Sweet dreams will be coming soon

So close your eyes and when you do,
know now and always

I love you

When it's time to turn out the light,

Give gentle kisses and say good night.

Tish Rabe has written over 170 books for Sesame Street, Disney, Dr. Seuss, and many more. She is a mom, a stepmom, and grandmother and is called "The Singing Author" by teachers because she SINGS to students during her school author visits. Tish is passionate about creating books that will help every child learn to read.

Gill Guile has illustrated over 600 books and written 50 of her own. Her breathtaking handpainted illustrations remind us of classic children's books. Gill lives in England with her husband and loves spending time with her family, painting, and playing tennis.